THE SUN WHISPERS, WAIT

Brown Turtle Poetry Series

THE SUN WHISPERS, WAIT

NEW AND COLLECTED POEMS

LUKE

BROWN TURTLE PRESS

For information, address
Brown Turtle Press, P.O. Box 44, Makanda, IL 62958
www.brownturtlepress.com

a publication of Brown Turtle Press

First published in the U.S.A. by Brown Turtle Press

11 10 09 08   4 3 2 1

Printed on recycled paper.♻

The paper used in this publication meets the minimum requirements of American National Standard for Information Sciences—Permanence of Paper for Printed Library Materials, ANSI Z39.48-1992. ∞

Some of the poems appearing in this volume were published in the following five anthologies: *The Missouri Poets* (Eads River Press), *Soda* (Quarter Press), *Quickly Aging Here* (Doubleday/Anchor), *Intro #2* (Bantam) and *Grand Fathers* (Henry Holt), and in the following periodicals: *America Magazine, Thought,* the *National Catholic Reporter, Callaloo, New Orleans Review, Ritual & Dissent, Yardbird Reader #4,* and *Studies in the Spirituality of Jesuits.* "Responding: A Blues Aesthetic" was published in *The Blues Aesthetic: Black Culture and Modernism* (Washington Project for the Arts). This volume includes the full text of *Accidental Grace* (published in the Callaloo Poetry Series, 1986).

The Judge William Holmes Cook Fellowship at Southern Illinois University Carbondale provided the funds for this book's publication. Brown Turtle Press gratefully acknowledges the university's support for its nascent publishing program.—Frank M. Chipasula, Founding Publisher.

For F. D. C., who saved my life,
so that I could find the healing words

CONTENTS

IV

V

INTRODUCTION

One October evening in 1957, while my father watched television, my mother cleaned the kitchen and my younger sister finished her homework, I lay on the living-room floor reading the current issue of *The Saturday Evening Post*. If the myth my mind has long nourished is at all accurate, I was reading a poem by Ogden Nash. After years of being fascinated by poetry found in my older sister's textbooks or in the heirloom books of my father's schooldays, I decided to see if I could imitate what I had been reading. When I finished my first attempt at versifying, I showed the result to my father. He handed it back to me, saying, "That's pretty good; you should keep doing that."

This volume appears a little over fifty years later, containing a life of my harvesting the seed planted in my imagination during my thirteenth year. The poems in this volume are, first of all, the pieces that Charles Rowell, the founding editor of *Callalloo* magazine prodded me to submit to him, when we were colleagues at the University of Virginia. Charles asked me why I had never published a book of poetry, and I replied, "no one ever asked me." He asked, and *Accidental Grace* appeared in 1986. Earlier, previously uncollected poems are also found here.

When I entered the Society of Jesus (the "Jesuits") in 1962, I was immersed into a culture as foreign to me as any I would have encountered at the far reaches of the planet. My being the only African American anywhere within sight, hearing or the affinity of the spirit, caused me many feelings of isolation and dislocation. My father sent me books, music, and my mother sent me letters. I wrote poems— because it was a way of talking to my *self*, and also a way of keeping at the practice of being an artist.

Some of those early poems were published and are collected here for the first time in over forty years.

My rearrangement of the old and new poems so that they engage in multiple levels of conversation, echo, embellishment and clarification, is an exercise of self-indulgence. But then poetry, like all art, is first and most importantly, *play*. Family, friends, acquaintances and brief encounters are the subjects of these pieces. In many ways the entire collection is a "dedication to itself." A friend of mine described my poems as the musings of "preternaturally wise twelve-year old."

Well, at least it is a voice; not always displayed, but present frequently enough to still spark a sense of enjoyment.

Why the name, "Luke"? Luke the Evangelist is remembered in the Roman Catholic liturgical calendar on the 18th of October. That is also the birthday of my father. A year after I began writing, I read an article about the traditions surrounding the devotion to St. Luke. He was a gentile among the Jewish "followers of the way." He was an artist in his use of Greek. His stories about the infancy of Jesus, his focus on the presence of Mary, the mother of Jesus, and his particular emphasis on the revelation of God to the small, forgotten and weak: this appealed to me. When I was encouraged to "take a name in religion" upon pronouncing my vows in the Society of Jesus, Luke was an obvious patron of what I already knew was a gift of mine. That his feast day was the same as my father's birthday was the compelling factor.

Early in my publishing career, as a way of honoring the saint and the progenitor, I decided to publish my poetry under this "pen name." Part of my teaching of African American culture and theology focuses on how each of us is called to define the terms by which we live. I remember the aesthetic ramblings of Gertrude Stein who made much of how nouns, being the names of things, carry much more authority than we sometimes recognize. One of the old songs of the enslaved Africans says, "I told Jesus it would be all right, if He changed my name..." This is an insight I took quite seriously.

Part of the tradition surrounding St. Luke is that he was also a painter who created a portrait of the mother of Jesus. It matters not at all whether such a postulation could be even remotely possible. He gave us sensitive pictures of shepherds, grieving parents, confused friends and acquaintances, hungry multitudes, and a man for whom words carried the weight of the world and eternity. Compassion, understanding, forgiveness and poetry were in the telling of the tales he recorded.

And my father said, "This is good. Keep doing it." It is a blessing that he gave me that advice, and that my mother—the original poet in the family—kept a dictionary by her chair for the sixty-two years that I knew her. Oh, I inherited words enough for the telling, even if the stories are most often whispered by and for the child within.

I

LORD KNOWS

lord knows honey
she said folding her hands
into the flowers of her apron
you got to make your
own road
           sometime

it was her wisdom
so i waited

coming and going
aint gonna do
when you get to be
old like me   just
going
       aint it like
some folks   to jump
on their own backs
stead of using the road
to get somewhere   fools
is fools   but you aint never been
one you hear
             sure gonna be hard
on your mama though
but she'll do all right
           now
before you go i wants to give you
a little something
           to help out
and i still have it

and the dollar bill
she unfolded slowly and put
into my hand

SOME FEW, SOME VERY FEW

some few, some very few, possess death
when it comes and hold onto it–
a daguerreotype displayed
next to their bed it becomes
a conversation piece referred to
as calmly as an ivory cameo bought
somewhere in switzerland

       this old woman–
the link for me to quantrill's raiders and
strawberries stolen the summer of 1889 and
hunger kept
on dusty shelves–

this old woman
took death into her body years ago
with quiet hospitality she understood
its need and could not refuse
though this new expense would
exhaust her small resources

she was once a large woman
a matriarch whose authority grew complete
as she buried two sisters four brothers
mother father six of her children

husband turned to the business
of her own funeral she has made
one last count of her household goods:
examined the soul of each survivor:
inventoried her life's decisions:
now she waits

while sewing a dress
from the remnant memories
of ninety years she says death
is cold to her: she does not like it

FOR MY GRANDFATHER

when I was your age
                      he said
there were books I loved to read
will you learn and find and read
them
          for me
                    of course yes today and
tomorrow if
              need
                    be all the fire
a promise feeds upon
                    I will yet
find and learn and love
what your blind eyes
                  can no longer
thaw

meanly then so small and foolish
were the words
                what does this
spell   and this and this
                    of coarse
small pebbles falling from the lips
this path was finely
              finally
                  stretched out
finding me
here
still sighting
          the adventure
you would never read again
old man

be patient as I turn
yet another
page

AT THE EDGE

my mother loses breath and nerve
as she watches my father resist all
aid and ease for death
                          his life is
devoured in larger doses daily without the rescue
                    of imagination he is
letting go of sound and wit and
serenity
              believing it to be a game
of interference he will not narcotize
his pain and it spills
                          onto us all
restless   angry   impotent and vain to
dream what will never be   he pushes
us
      to dwell at the edge of a dwindling
fire   a draining river   and stare
her bewildered hands scream out and
grab her children
                        she would marry
him and bear his sons   she will
grieve when he is gone
                            but she cannot
rest   hearing him now   unable to replace
pain with peace
                      and she does not know
how to scold him to go to sleep for fear
that he would at last obey

HOME VISIT AT CHRISTMAS

i wonder do you sit there for all
time   waiting to be seen in the light
we bring
              revealed in prophecy
uncovered by idle drunken sons
the shame of death   discovered
stranger   erasing your hardness
height and flesh
                    i look at your
hands
          hands that pulled us into
traffic   into crowds   curses
giants   monstrous shadows   all
too fierce and inarticulate
to withstand
                except we were
pulled through them gently
roughly   with—at the last—
dispatch as each new son was
ready to be flung out into wind

the pattern stayed
the delicacy disappeared

your hands now tremble matches
drop bits and crumbs   ignore
the simplest string and button
lay soft and tired on your chair

if you would
motion to me now   this second
i would take your touch in gentle
gratitude
              but where could i take
you   what could i show you in this
world i still fear

                    and would you
come with me   if i asked
                            my nakedness
was your last great humor   yours has
become my penitence and drought
i am no guide for you
i cannot bear your gaze
your fading life brushes
across my heart and
drives
me into flight
                    you are mute
having packed your words away
and i am dumb   in need still
of my private roots
                            and
the children we hold between
us shake out our grasp so soon

STORIES ABOUT CHRONE

I

looks like chrone the care-
taker got careless
          again
when the lights went out last night
seems like he was rooting around
his junkroom and put in the wrong
size bulbs
       folks say chrone
ain't had his mind on duty since
his boy ran away and got killed
overseas (or down south
             folks
ain't sure which as if it mattered
anymore)
      when you been here
awhile you learn to overlook his
crazy ways since they never hurt
nothing no way
        this time is rich
them lights make the whole neighbor-
hood look cleaner   like they burn
some of the dirt away
         and the trees
look painted almost and the glare
is making the snow melt weeks
sooner than it ought to
        chrone
got the knack of messing in the
good with the crazy sure enough

II

ain't nobody never called him

nothing but chrone
                              once my daddy
said he found a letter dropped
by the doorstoop sent to mister
chronostheos eupater
                              daddy says
anybody called   chrono-the-os
you-payter must have a black
mama and a jew daddy
                              who else
would think up a name like that

some of us was sitting on
the roof talking about chrone
i don't believe he is the janitor
he really owns the place
                              and just
pretends to be a forgetful old
wino   i bet he's got money and
stuff everywhere
                              rotting and
stinking because he can't remember where he hid it
                              probably
saving it for his son and won't
admit his boy's been dead for
years
              they told me i was just
dreaming
                    i'm going to look
for it someday   somebody ought
to get some use out of it
                              cause
when chrone dies the government
will take it all anyway

chronostheos eupater: "*God of time, the Benevolent Father.*"

III

i wonder why he wears a
wool sweater even on a hot
day
     my grandma said it's
just that he's old   older
than abraham
          and daddy said
yeah   and he taught the snake
how to
     crawl
        and been cold
ever since

IV

sitting here on the steps one
night   the air pulled back
           like
when at supper everybody gets real
quiet because daddy's in one of his
moods   liable to slap you silly if you
ask for water too loud
         and i had this
deep feeling of wanting to run off
some place alone
       when grandma started
singing one of her church songs in
the bedroom   shouting she could sing
because she's happy
        and the air stretched
out and i stopped needing to run

just then the basement door cracked
open
     chrone didn't come out or move
or nothing
      and i couldn't see him

through the space   so i sat there
and let grandma sing on in my head
it kept the night breathable
                                    maybe
chrone had the same idea

V

my last summer of being real little
about three years ago
                                    this boy named
Raven had to live with us
                                    grandma tried
to explain how he was her people and mine
he was her baby sister's daughter's nephew
I think
                    and somebody killed somebody else
and Raven couldn't stop crying
                                    and grandma
was the one who had a way with deathcrying children
so he was in my bed snuffling and kicking
he smelled sour all the time but with some burnt-
wood smoke mixed in with sweetgrass
                                            that first
night in the dark   I asked him where he was born

he said
                    I born in Legba Mississippi
                                            but we moved
to Toomsuba two years ago

next day when I told Daddy he said
                                    boy shoulda stayed
where he was born when you leave Legba some part
of the house is always dusty
                                    Daddy was peculiar about
Raven even before he came to us
two weeks into his visit one afternoon a Friday
while I was sitting on the steps with Chrone watching

nothing but the heat get dirtier
                    Raven come running down
the steps he stopped turned back to the door screaming
in a scratchy whispery scream
                         then he cursed at grandma
who was standing in the doorway holding her white
leather bible on her bosom
                         my throat closed off
and I tried to stand up
                    when Chrone pushed me back
to the step

          come here you   Raven   he said
real quiet real quiet slow quiet come here

I said
          when Raven turned his wild look on Chrone
every sound left the street I know it did

then Chrone said
                    you done two things wrong son
you showed your behind to a good woman and you
tarnished sunlight with your tongue
                              now stop
and he slapped him
                    deep hard and final
this aint nowhere you ever been
nor will it be
                    I stopped being real little
the next day when Grandma made me give Chrone
fifty cents wrapped in one of them stiff lilac-
smelling handkerchiefs she got every Mothers Day
from the deacons of the church
                         tell him to buy him
some wine

was all she said

II

HAIKU

I

The pine trees explode
the birds at dawn and cradle
their exclamations

II

Our house stores sunlight
in baskets and sets it out
for the evening fire

III

The small drunk turtle
challenges the morning wind
to race to the pond

JUNE RAIN

A girl
with a smile from Gauguin
strides barefoot
through the 8 a.m. downpour
carrying her books
like a melon.

The sky is bullied by the wind
while umbrellas
hide the fact
and call it cloudburst.

I think I will stand
here at the corner
and watch the steaming street
slow traffic   and wait to see
if children still
wear yellow raincoats.

1965

PROCESSIONAL

The darkness of night, God, their constant hungering
summon the keen-edged monks to walk their souls around
and through and down the pillars of the cloister.

Come by clanging bell at nine-fifteen, the solemn
march of folded arms
echoes the autumn drift of leaves; the sound
of fine white sand swept across a desert moon,
or over bones
of cenobites who lie beneath the ageless dust;
who, similarly, stripped their souls for heaven
with repentant tears.

The slow, recurring rhythm makes suspensive years
while formless shadows move before each other—one
by one sweeping with his habit's hem his sand,
his rubble heap of one more day complete, illumined
in the starlight: grains of unasked questions, unknown
whys clotted by a lack of time, a lack of will, an
answer still unseen in the cold, mosaic moonlight
checkering the black, processing silhouettes.

Each moving figure drops his feet upon the tracks
of those who went before. (Back as far as
recollection shuffled the bare, rough feet of men
stiffened by the coldness of the stones
seeping through the calloused skin, mocking woolen robes,
and chilling the thin, starved marrow of their bones.)

In the heavy stillness of the monastery night,
the men of prayer walk silently at nine-fifteen.
and the stone-paved moonwashed cloister walk
is ground down to fineness
while grains of sand are bleached by cold moonlight.

1965

20

WIND BELLS

every now and then the little brass bells
brought to me by a friend from india
who knows the mind to be a sometimes invalid
shudder   startled by the adagio afternoon breeze

but that is fanciful
those brass leaves secured
upon their limb at the edge
of my forest belong there
hanging in the air

and never show surprise
they are cast in peace

eventually the screams of villages soak
into the yellow earth beside the ganges
the saffronrobed priests marked with sandalwood
continue in silent centuries of prayer
and everywhere the grey sick cattle keep their vigils

if life were to turn suddenly on its straw mat
and die during the night these small brass bells
would tremble every now and then but not
not in surprise

OUTSIDE SUBIC BAY

the large birds scream and search endless
hours on the thick air
                                silent only when
the rain of the monsoon season whips
even the trees into a whimpered crouch

god has made the monsoon   a purging
tool of summer   god has the scavenging
birds for his net

alone in this room in this wind and
in this rain
                    and in this country of
the crying amputated beggars the thought

of a god who hurls the wide throated storm
upon me   scratches my skin my eyes
my memory of you
                                outside subic bay

SPIRIT GATES : A CELEBRATION

for John Scott, who has forged gates by which we visit all our worlds

1.

Tonight, at midnight almost exactly the sirens in Louisville began cutting
a way into the wet cottony air;
the old man in the next room sends cigar smoke and hungerings
into my window.
No one with a name knocks on the door, my fingers
search for no comfort; no.

Are children, in some land settling into dreams of pinescented hills,
stripping leaves for the sun bleached streets, layered upon the parkways
where we drive, eternally?

It is Palm Sunday in Kentucky.

Jesus is looking for a crowd to adore him, bleed him, set him
cypress bound and scaled to our bitter size.

The spring flowers in the graveyards suck perfume from the sighs
of sagging moonhaunted clouds.

2.

When the baby got sick restless fretful in not sleeping no more,
Uncle Joe started doing road work—for a bed
a baby's bed he said—where lil'Bit could sleep peaceful;
then for the rent money—Lord, how the man wants
his money, 'fore he puts us all out on the street
and then bed or no bed—it will be a truly fretful
time around here, around here for us all.

But it was the dawn time when he would glide
around in the shadows putting out flowers, making bread
and lemonade from the lemons he hoarded in from Florida;
it was the dawn time when I heard him whispering
to Aunt Maymee, like she was still alive, still
laying in that bed looking at him, eating him with
her sighing laughing eyes;

It was the dawn time, when he was sneaking surprises
into near most every corner of the house
                                                    that he went
on the road to make payment on–

3.

Across the street two buildings down in the basement
this little boy lives with his mama she always be
picking up things in the street off the steps everywhere
made a dress once out of some curtains Miz Joyce gave her
got petunias growing in coffee cans old scotch bottles rubber tires
probably make roses grow in that red clay dirt if she wants
                                                    the boy don't play
much with the kids on this block seem to sit too much in the corner
for my business
and he got quiet drinking eyes see everything even before it turns the corner
but I guess he must think I'm just as crazy in my ways

                                        with the arthritis
in my hands and my bad circulating blood I'm at this window more than I'da
ever thought

as good a woman as the mama act she must not cook too much or something
little boy can smell my supper from across the street in a basement I tell you
long about sun settling he out there walking the curb looking for the smell
of greens or hot grease ready to grab some chicken or that sour bite of twice
rising rolls in the oven
                            but he got the ways of an old man   I wonder
whose soul took up with him when he was born he gets to my steps and just
sets down
                    sometimes he takes a coat hanger or
some sorta found wire or even
old paper sacks and twists away his fingers trying to make some words stand stiff
in the last light of the day

I don't shame him with a full plate maybe a piece of cornbread or
a teacup of greens or a wing some little bits like I ain't even studying
about his old self
                        since I'm eating in the twilight window
and he keeps finding my steps   it just seem what you
ought to do

he always leaves his words of wire and paper on the steps when
he starts off again

                    moving down the curb squinting for something to keep

they pretty on the kitchen window ledge   they real pretty for a child

4.

Since Christmas Mama seems to be failing
I know it was Daddy's passing right after the weather turned
so bad

her hands seem lost no meals to fix no tea to help him sip from
a spoon

no real holding or touching his face his hands his neck

                              she stays
in bed most of the day sometimes getting weak from the distraction

two days ago I come by to get her up and into the
kitchen for a noon
meal

while we were sitting there the high sun heat up our feet
she says to me I just saw your daddy walk past the door
                            did you
see
him or am I going crazy did you see him did you
                        oh lord in
heaven
I thought I don't even want to know where she is getting
slapped
in the night or who is
humming in the hallway early in the morning
                           I almost
fainted when Miss Joyce came up the steps soon after
mama said all that

I remember sitting here some Saturday nights when
Mama was all dressed up

with that pretty cologne of hers making the kitchen smell
like the parlor
at Easter waiting on Daddy to bring the car up to the gate
so they could
step out
                    dancing all the night long she would
move like honey on warm bread
I would get a hurting all inside holding my joy and my
breath squeezing
my eyes to hold her in the light

then Daddy would step to the door   she would turn and
throw me a kiss
for the night time
                        and move to his waiting hand

her eyes are following him moving with the elm tree
shadows on the porch

and then they would slip out the door whispering
swaying to each other's
song
            Mama you ain't crazy I said   and my tea went ice
cold with a taste of grit

O'HARE : WAITING ROOM

I

they sit hunched over
paper and plastic bags
bending into each other
in the airport
uncertain of how they might
fly and will anyone
smell
the fear instead
of the bleach and starch
they have applied
heart soul mind

and strength
for the journey
to Winchester
to attend

Aunt Georgia's passing

II

intermittent sun flashes
across the lobby while
I read

this is the haunting: black man
with stomach
gently curved outward
for the sheer comfort
of having put in
28 years at the Ford plant
of having found the fit
at last

       in the night hollow
lying next to him all these
years
       sits dreaming
in the early Sunday sunlight
with hand solid on

the flesh
       that warrants
for each of us
heart's grief and ache
fingers drumming a song
no one will ever hear

sung

A POEM FOR NOLA FIFE

a bouquet of ninety-five roses

Some loveliest of the roses
trace the fences of this block
long limbs of red and white and salmon pink
swollen with heated scent and dust
droop into my path
as I walk   looking for surprises in the street

And I am taken
to the country summers
of days when forever came and went
by noon   by supper
                    by fireflies
conversing in the fields and yards

At this window tonight
as I drift and nod soothed with tea
sweetened by sudden recollections
(the surprise of our still being here)
the faces and voices of some of the loveliest
of my life sway and beckon
me to sleep

                I am comforted
by the roses I have touched
those that have gifted my window vase
my mind   my heart

where fireflies forever
dance their signatures in light

A BOOK OF PROVERBS : FRAGMENT

I have been saying this
in a light to the head
dizzy way
             for the joke

but the truth will slam you
like a brick out the sky

just the same

the only children I know
come already wrapped
so I don't hear me being called
daddy   no time soon

it will surely drain

meaning
me
and my bank account

THERE'S A MAN GOING ROUND . . .

Mama Lilly said we ought to tell people not to call
our house past nine any night
when folks are sick

they might think the call is for them
and try too hard to answer the sounding
bell

She didn't need to tell
me

I can't even stand to have no
body knock on the door past
supper time

It might be somebody
I don't even need to know

A QUESTION OF NETS

Does Jesus really go fishing
on Saturdays?

That's what I heard.

Uh-huh, that sure is the
truth.

Every Saturday that
the Good Lord allows.

No wonder I can
never
catch him.

A MEDITATION ON STANDARDS

Just after school yesterday when
the sun made parts of the house seem
like they were fading
                              Grandmama was in
the kitchen peeling potatoes and humming
about "something within I cannot explain"

I was working on my 5s and 6s

and Poppa was just looking
—like he mostly does now—

And the doorbell rang

It was two white boys in white
shirts and black pants

I told Poppa and he said, "hunh."
I told Grandmama and she quick
checked the calendar (nothing was due
for another three days)
                              she slowed down
her peeling, some,
                        "see what they want.
From the porch, now. I ain't in the mood,
today. You hear?" Poppa said, "hunh," again.

They were from the college down by the river.
Were we interested in hearing about Jesus? Did
we need a program to help us?
                            I looked in the
kitchen. Poppa looked at me. Hard. "Well, well, well."
I don't know who said that. Maybe we all did.

And then, whispering like a match striking the side
of the box,

Poppa said, "Lucilla, He's got the whole world in his hands."

I let them into the house.

LETTER

an experience in which a personage, thing, or event appears
vividly or credibly to the mind, although not actually
present, under the influence of a divine or other agency:
a vision. does it always start with a vision? how long
must you wait before you can call it a vision?   and what did
you see?
              i saw myself sitting on the top of a high mountain,
with my back leaning against a brilliant moonwhite cross.
from the base of the mountain all the way to the crest
line were thousands of people who were stretching towards
me. and i, sitting there spent, reached out my arms—as
a shadow of the cross—toward them.
                              and during the space
of one year, i saw this four times.   and now when i think
of it, i see just as clearly as the first time it came to
me. was this the look of the still voice that socrates
heard? was this the chalice of jesus at gethsemane? was
it even a vision?   how do you test it out?   i have told
three experts about "my dream" and none of them ever gave
me more than a funny look and a long silence.
                              and we have
been trained to sort out even the silences in our lives.
so, if you please, distinguish. it was real. right. it
fits. it works. eight years of waiting has sifted the
hard, clean grains of my life. they exist. but are they
named? can they be named?   of course they can be
named.   managed understood tamed. if we do it just do it
doing it always tames the unknown give god a name   his future
is ours and we are his people. the words. magic is in
the words.   always for me in the words.   and in the silence.
the long silence.   to be broken.   the silence? no.   me.
i am to be broken.   wasn't that an obvious clue to it all.
be broken.   the hard grains of your life are sifted through
the silence.   and you must be pieced out to be spilled.
and they will come and feed upon you.   if your strength is
hard and clean and full of blood, the hungry will smell it

and come to eat.   be the lamb of god.   roasted. at least
properly dressed and quartered.

                                    to perform the sacred rites
especially the sacrificial offerings. walk down the street
in north st. louis and that will be enough.   call yourself
priest over cocktails and see.   hunger and desperation.
the offering of sacrifice.   even if you are imagining it,
when you say this is my body and this is my blood, the
identification stays.   and stays and after all they were
your words that everybody heard.   roasted lamb.   of god
and of the people.   god is everywhere.   and so is hunger.
you saying so simplifies matters.

my talent is to die.   but not cheaply.   to die for the best
possible price.   on a mountain for a crowd.   lift up the
sins of the world. i have lifted them up.   lift up your
heart. i have lifted it up on a spit. a tree branch forked
and spearsharp. lifted up.   in silence.   at last i can
name it.   sursum corda.   the witness of dying.   the show
the ritual the teaching of the people to lift up their
hearts in hunger.   at last i face the question which for
years has had no word to bring it flesh.   what is my priest-
hood.   to live the vision and be lifted up.   by god.   for
the people.   my gift and my service is not to perform works.
no i was sitting beneath the cross.   it is not to speak.
the poetry of this world is silence and the asceticism of
option that we cannot exercise.   i can speak
therefore i will not.   i can give life therefore i will
not. i can rule therefore i will not.   i can construct an
answer that will satisfy therefore i will not.

                                    the gift of
knowledge that i have shared has been time.   the only gift
an artist has is time and the magic of controlling time.
if you know me you cannot escape the twisted heart that is
broken by wine and heroin and loneliness.   and the breaking
will point where it will where it must.   the endurance of
never leaving the edge of the knife.   choose life therefore
choose the vision.   i offer in my hands the body of jesus
broken by chaos and fear devoured by hunger and lonely

nights.   it is the gift that god placed before me and i have
taken it up and said this is my body and my blood.   if
you will not touch it can you turn away.   if you avoid the
gift will you live your vision.   the poverty of this world
denies any choice in the matter.   what the lord gives you
receive.   change your diet or starve to death.   evolve
and grow.   choose life and be new.   wine.   hearts of flesh.
men.   a man called and chosen from among men to offer
sacrifice.   to offer men as sacrifice.   to lift up what we
have been gifted.

what will i do.   nothing.   you need me
for nothing except priest.   the priest for the sacrifice.
you are the sacrifice and someone must prepare you.   and
you know it.   the vision is yours.   the people are all of
us.   all of our building and striving will fail to satisfy
because we are not asked to build or construct.   we are
asked to sacrifice and witness to lift ourselves up as
offering for the people.   and how are we to do this.   find
your heart and break it like bread and let them feed upon
it.   for they are hungry.   and will you survive.   if you
remember who you are and why you were chosen.   to be reminded
to accept time and cast off fear.   the strength of our life
must be a vision.   and do you have a vision.   you have me
and all i have is the sense of a vision.   so now we know.
now we have a word for it now we have the magic.   begin.
please begin.   we are masters of the ritual and we must
begin or no one will know.

III

EVENING NEWS : ST. LOUIS

willard wirtz, secretary of labor,
supports humphrey the news says
over in central illinois
the big muddy was reported
to crest safely under flood level
because of recent heavy rains
snow flurries with slight precipitation
were predicted for st. louis
johnson received an ovation
in st. patrick's cathedral
a late bulletin announced
that martin l. king was shot
to death tonight on a balcony
in memphis
there were 3,238 vietcong
killed last month by allied forces
mrs. mabel burnham won $630
in the kxok easter egg contest
the pope still declines to make a statement
on birth control

4 April 1968

THE TOMB OF IGNATIUS : ROME

1.

mark it out: six footsteps. just under
that. deep enough for a child
for a child to hide   and if able to stretch
and turn over   it would touch the walls.
no more room.
not even air would be comfortable beyond
these limits.   and tightly sealed.

2.

see it: a boat
a covered gold boat   shaped
to float lightly into the sea   riding
high off to the edge of nowhere
if called.   or sent.

3.

angels everywhere.   pulling the eye
up and around.   pointing into corners where
prayer evaporates and silence lingers.
behind marble clouds and silver folds
bronze curving in and out   the breath
that comes from the holy places everywhere
you look.   can you see it.
now.   mark it.   out.

4.

when the bones have been cleaned they must be
boiled until the last scraps of meat and muscle
collect on top.   boil them in lye for the
best results

5.

results are seldom expected.   even though
you know that plants need water
and rich dirt for successful growth   once
in awhile   a seed has been found
to take root in dust   airless dust
dust that is sealed away from
light   from rain   from everything but
memory
       (and even some times in forgotten
dust)

6.

we were wrong   distracted   fools
after gold to believe that visions
come in silence
         though a busload of belgian
tourists buying postcards   avès riding
in a wave of mumbled music   timed by
camera shutters and lights locked in
15 minute cycles
        the vision in that should
have been a clue

7.

that he would have accepted

everything at once
how clear he knew that
not even bernini himself could contain
an italian determined on devotion

8.

little child

ignatius
who could follow a lame man
who wept more and more as
time slipped him somewhere.
beyond the child.
and back again

9.

called.   or sent.
the eye cannot be held to silver
lights the perfect draping on an
angel's thigh
                    it is drawn to wonder
if the dust
has any hidden

10.

sustenance

11.

it could
it could

12.

something brought us here

13.

mark it.   nowhere.   mark it out.
see.   somewhere.   see it.   dust.
gold and bronze.   tears.   visions
called it.   out.
                    sustenance.
sent.   sent or called.   called.

and sent.   sent and called.   here.
yes here.   of course here.   he
would know.
                    he knew.   a flame
is always certain.
                            especially
in darkness.   in silence.   here.
yes here.
                    sustenance.   in dust.
in tears.   in tourists.   lights.
and visions.   yes.   mark it.
everywhere.

5 YEARS LATER : FOR US (FOR MARTIN)

1.

ain't a soul amongst us
who don't know for sure
LORD, LORD.   that we ain't
in heaven yet
and our hell is standing still

did you hear him shout
don't you get weary
don't you get weary

2.

like as not we all old
folks   bent and twisted
from the common misery
shading our eyes with
crooked fingers   palm-
high to the sun
                    looking
out down the road all day
who are we looking for

did you hear him shout
soon I will be done with
the troubles of the world,
with the troubles of the world

did you hear him children
did you

3.

so much time lost

since I heard him shout
since I heard him sing
since I heard him pray
since he died at supper
and they took him away from us

4.

some nights, dark and quiet, I get to nodding
my head thinking and listening once more to
his big, spirit-filled voice urging us on
urging us on to victory
                              then my hand starts
tapping on my knee and my eyes jerk open
straining to see him up there on his mountain
pointing out the dream   pointing out
                                           so much
time lost   since I heard him shout

5.

sometimes the tears still come
sometimes I catch myself looking
out the window for a sign in the sky
or something clear and certain

and what I see is that wagon
that wagon pulled by them
mules   and all of us all of
us LORD. pushed down into grief
where there are no words   stumbling
after
          hoping just to make it

6.

So much time lost
my faith is slow rumbling
like that wagon and I'm

tired, LORD, LORD. I'm
tired
     of trying to hear him
trying to forget him   I'm tired
of so much time lost   of quick
pains in my hands and knees
tired of the shooting flashes
in my head
         LORD, LORD. we standing
here   it seems   where he left us
looking out at jordan
               waiting
for the signal to begin   waiting
for what
      I heard him say keep
a-moving on   I know I heard
him say it

7.

is he crying like we are now
over so much time lost

our tears seem to make the
jordan swell its banks

weariness don't you stop
me   I heard him say it
LORD, LORD.   I heard him
shout
     so much time lost
we still got today
         LORD. DO
RIGHT, JESUS. let us take
the plunge
       we ain't so
broken yet that we can't
move a mighty distance more

8.

shout it children   shout it
for him
make jordan shrink and tremble
and move a mighty distance
more

like we heard him say

we still got today
shout it children
shout it

PHOTOGRAPHS : ATLANTA 1980–1981

1.

in some parts of the city even the dirt
is tired
        shuffled over   stomped on
swept flat   hard as a gravestone
it does not give to the step
                    so
men grow tired from walking on it

their aching legs get heavy as the sun
lowers its own hot weight to their shoulders
bearing down
                bearing down   and the dirt
resists   throwing back the shadows it
drains of moisture and tint
                    remaining still
dry
    still hard
            and dry
                and implacable

2.

what trees there are   stretched thin
with hate   ignore each other
                    distantly
offering the weakest of branch   the slightest
of shade   pitiless to childish claims
of flickering peace   refuge   and cover

no old men lean under them
to recollect their purpose and their breath
no old women strip the leaves and the bark
for medicine
                the trees disdain to line

the land   the fields   or the foothills of
the northern range
                    like the sparse jagged
teeth of some mythic prowling jackal
                                    the trees
make wide and slashing wounds wherever they rip
into the middle sky

3.

down there   beyond the fence was a creek
once
        where the thicker brush and the high
weeds seem close
                        their closeness is the only
sign
the rain might stay for two or three days
just enough to glut their roots and give
a beggar's sustenance

the children will slip off there now and
again and come back scratched and scared

they have to learn themselves that lesson
since no yelling ever gets through

4.

nobody knows how old she really is

if there was a shade tree she wouldn't care
for it
        has to be moved into the sun so that
she can feel it on her eyes
                            (they got cloudy
years ago)
            when you get near you can smell
the cinnamon and smoke and lye that mingles
in her sweat

she sits there hours every day
fingering that rag until holes are worn into it
calls herself looking out for the children
                                        but
they slip away
            they slip away
                        leave here for
good

brought one boy back last month looking
like life had squeezed him hungry

she reached out and stroked his face
                        and smiled
a little
        it was about all the sign you could
expect

THERE MUST BE A SOURCE

there must be a source of music somewhere
that plays inside the heads of these young girls
who walk so
        softly   so softly
             the long thin arms
moving easily with a slow swing brushing against
the also thin hard legs that partly pace
            partly march
like cats brown black and soft young girls
with the firm look of untested flesh
          that music
must be sad that they hear from somewhere
because they walk so softly and with a sureness
of time that no one ever learns but is with them
from somewhere
      and always
        one of them plays
her woman game with a boy on the street and
there are no words just a moment made old
because her eyes tell him his body is good
and young and untested and he knows
        and
she quietly easily slaps his face with
gentleness
     holding him to her for just a pulse
they are intimate and understanding here on
the corner and they both move to a music that
comes from inside
      a music that no one that young
could know
     which means that inside
they are old and it is another world that
has made them old
      and given them this music
which is soft   and it is sad

ABOUT A MONTH AGO

about a month ago
                          this ugly old
dog took up with us   sleeping on
the front porch   and following us
around with the most mournful
look
            nobody paid him no mind or
fed him or petted him
                          we just
walked around him and ignored
him like some old grease smell
that stays and stays in the
kitchen
              after awhile i started
feeling kind of sorry for him

too old to move much   he just
laid there   i dont know   maybe
he was too old to feel sorry
for and just wanted some peace
                             we
found that dog dead in the street
yesterday
             and i started looking
around this place thinking about
why i stay
              lord knows it cant be
my pedigree

WHEN THE EAGLE FLIES : ST. LOUIS

the only right time for jesus to walk
in this city would be on friday night
because that's when the people are so
sad and loud and running around
and jumping and dancing and scared
like hell that somebody will see that
they're scared and wipe them off the earth
with understanding   that jesus could
do some good
                  but he wont be walking
the streets in this town because from
what i hear it's not safe and there
are too many loudtalking niggers and
soursouled white folks for jesus to
get to and comfort even if he had
all the time in heaven which
is what this place needs and aint
and everybody   even jesus   knows it

THE ARCH : ST. LOUIS

1.

we are coming back to it
the taste of cold air edged like
a blade, bitterness slicing
our throats   lancing our eyes
of salt
            drawing off the heart
the last film of hope we suffered
under
            the death of men
the rooting of despair in the few
(even the world is few when one
man you have known lifts his head
finally away from you
                        and is silent
forever)
            survivors locked in trying
to understand

2.

the crying is heard whenever a shadow
resists the need for sun
the crying is felt in the muscles along
the back, the neck, the arms held ready
to lift, to hold, to take away
                        (even
the world, if known, is lifted when one
man is carried into the earth)
                        our last
link   desperately clung to for difference

3.

and yet
our hearts continue beating
the icy breath gulped in anguish
feeds the blood

and allows us the strength to stumble
until we are able
to walk

4.

we are coming back to it
we are coming back to it
we are coming back

5.

the sleeping spirit surges
up like oil

6.

we are all coming
back to it
it is all coming back

7.

those who possess the city sought
to claim their right forever
                and
pulled out of the earth out of
the flat land/breasted river
                   the
silver ribbon
          to tremble in

the reflected moonlight and muddy
brown water

8.
no flags are left
from the north the river brings whispers
it is the whisper of our return
it is the shaking loose of dirt by skeletons
of the hunt

9.

for the voice of the spirit

SILAS BLUE EAGLE OF ROSEBUD

He is chief
         only in the summer
    when tourists
            come to strip his headdress
      and dangle the feathers
         from their rear-view mirrors

    The chamber of commerce
                can verify
   his lineage
      (and do so
    on the back of a postcard)

The blood of Sitting Bull and Red Cloud
    has been tamed
         they say
    and the chief
      will pose for pictures
          every morning
for a very slight fee

GOOD FRIDAY IN OMAHA : NIGHT

flat white pills given out at the county
clinic will short circuit the pain
                                    from
the plate in the thigh to the busted knee-
cap down to the shattered ankle
                                        the flat-
iron hotel will for five dollars plus tax
let you sleep in a plain room for one night
not let you bathe
                        not give you clothes that
need no pins to be kept decent
                                    the happy cab
company will send a young black driver to pick
you up
        and relieve the need to slide back
down the hill   your arms too weak to push
and steady the castaway crutches from st.
vincent de paul
                        and i will turn off my tape
recorder's hurting sound   silence bessie
smith's lesson for tonight and listen to
you
        that much can be done   and with such
dispatch that it seems a shame no one
knows how to get you back to scottsbluff
no one knows how to speed your pension
papers up
                no one knows   except maybe for
bessie how to answer your last slurred
question
                what do you do in the meantime
what do you do in the mean time
                                        i don't
know how to sing you a blues   it was just
my night to be on duty

FOR A FRIEND RETURNING TO ROSEBUD RESERVATION

if you cannot explain your return
they will not teach you   it is not
their way
                they will invite you   and
sit with you   walking in the fields
at sunset they will notice you
stumble hungrily in the canyons
they will move aside
                                parting like
wind in the pine clusters they will
touch you
                yes that is their way
touching
                did you think that you
took nothing away when you left
before   did you remember the
whistling in the darkness   the
water rustling in the lake
                                did
you find the thin purple and the
grey mist and the sand brown light
driving on any highway into the
west or south
                the sand scratched
at your skin   the air stuck to you
and the empty sky cleared your
vision
                they will not teach you
they will wait for you staring and
smiling   singing the wordless songs
offering you space
                                they will wait
for you to be chilled inside your
lungs and ask for a place near
the burning fire
                they will not

teach you   but they will give you
time enough to learn how
                              the hills
slide into the river without fear

THE PRIESTS OF ROSEBUD

have an accidental grace to no
longer fear the circle of their
beginning
to know the people of these plains
in courtesy   not wrath

but there is a curse with power in
the wind and rain and thunder

to die for what they believe
would be a blessing
to beg browbeat or threaten god
for signs and wonders   would make
them heirs of the golden-colored
saints that hang upon their walls

but the connection has died within
them
          these priests are orphans
of their history
                    the people will
not kill them   the people look
away to salvage their pride

the people give them gifts
of crowd and circumstance

this new martyrdom is the losing
of the center   the absence of an
end to doubt   the daily taste
of smallness
                    the people stay fixed
and the priests of rosebud move from
place to place praying for deliverance

THE BURIAL OF PEARL WALKING EAGLE AT ROSEBUD

wide standing clouds held still
by the dakota sun offer me no shade
strings of heat web   weave and hook
a net that catches us struggling
like fish pulled   gasping for air
from the sea
                    and we do not move
arranged as lodge poles around
the gravesite   we are attentive
in our steaming silence
                            the wind
is soft and warming   the ground
is hot   the grass   where it grows
among the gravel and the sand
defies the dryness

the walking eagle woman
                            is free
of us   and is burdened now by
only the mound of earth and
plastic flowers
                    for nothing
flourishes here but resignation

wild heaped and brittle splotches
the flowers will not die
they will not fall   (the air is
much too gentle)
                        i learn that
 reverence stands still
                            and the
sharp keening of her daughter is
the only prayer with the power
to cut through us all and beyond
the vast prairie to breaks
without an echo

CHRISTMAS : ST. LOUIS

before you get the house in order   the tree-
lights untangled   and all your packages wrapped
and labeled   i thought i should write and tell
you that jesus was already seen this year by
a friend in the middle of a crowd at a stop-
light downtown

                               he was in a greyhound bus headed
for chicago

                  my friend waved but jesus did not
seem to notice him he was staring at the sky
and he looked very tired and sad   my friend
said   we should let everybody know before they
waste a lot of time shopping and cleaning and
getting ready that jesus has come and gone
to another city

WHAT KIND OF WORLD

what kind of world
is it indeed that forces
christmas to our winter
and some poor ragged jesus
to stumble over starved dead
rotting in the jungles
to steel himself against
shouts of men behind
stone walls and take upon himself
a cold world and fall again
in his still fruitless coming

we have never fully
understood what kind of world
it is indeed
              we have
in our land this winter
a famine of simplicity:
homes
food
magnificent hallelujahs
for a hundred resurrections
and a thousand births
but no straw
no animals
no shepherds struck
dumb with fear and wonder
no virgins
no silent and adoring kings

no not this year   i
do not want a savior's coming
our nights are neither quiet
calm   nor bright   we have
everything to keep us living
and go about collecting

scraps of mute despair
to stuff in window cracks
and under doors to keep away
our loneliness
this biting awful cold
what kind of world
is it indeed
wait awhile   sweet
jesus   just a year
to give us time
just a year   to give
us time
          but you will come
i know: you must
you will come now
in this dead
and barren world
and stumble
and be cold
and grow more ragged
and more poor until
gasping blood   you spit
your anguish into the dry earth
and cry to be delivered

and you will
and we will
and they who come
after us will

this winter waiting
is our ritual
it must be carried out
even though we
no longer keep the mystery
of our fathers

give us time

perhaps a year
will bring us mysteries
and we may beg
a savior's coming

UPON WHICH TO REJOICE

A slight stirring darkness
ordered us to hesitate.
Somehow we had found it.
The hard earth was matted with brittle hay;
the soaked-in acid smell of animals
stifled us in the first instants;
rough branches of juniper
scratched against the mud walls.
The night was cadenced
with the warm heavy breathing
of a woman who has borne a son
and, resting from her labor,
looks upon her child.

We had not surprised them
or disturbed their night.
Unmistakably
they had expected us and we,
in turn, had sensed they would be there.

No one spoke,
which made the stillness reverence;
while provision for her comfort
became our awkward male concern:
adding to the fire, another cloak,
tethering animals. He took
our embarrassment with gentle
eyes and helped us do again
what he had done before we came.

But we had nothing else to give
and our silence was inadequate,
though none of us knew why.

A LEGEND OF CARAVANS

as if the human mind could not hold
the shock of wise men worshiping
the irony was molded into a legend
of caravans led by kings
                        and we
could be content with gold
and the smoke of rich spices except
the equal play of chance in myth
gave to one the blackness of night
to wear as he knelt before a cave
offering a judgment
                    (for one who would be
king who would be wise   who must be
god and man to hold the heavy
weight of gold   to savor adoration)
knowing his was the last
the bitterness gift   of sorrow

DELIVER INTO US

St. Louis, 1971. The Search for Charles Hale

first in rain   then snow   through the fire-
chewed ruins of the northside deserted by
everything but cold rotting air
                                                    police and
city volunteers hunt for a missing child
                                                           keeping
us informed   to nothing definite   the news reports
feed our strained hope with some slight signs
each day
                  and each night   the ageless silence
that is always with us   scratches our minds
like a desert wind   and we   like forgotten
nomads scattered in some dark countryside   crawl
close and cling to whatever light we have
                                                 visited
with this   the listening city stirs before it
sleeps waiting restless   without peace
distracted   and caught in time
                                         until this child
is found   declared seen   or delivered into us

WITH TOMORROW STRETCHED OUT

when the kings had gone   taking
with them the last echo of tambourine
and harness into the shifting deserts
of their dreams
                    after the silent nomads
had finally straightened themselves
from their unexpected   awkward   homage
and gone searching for their scattered
herds and some shred of meaning
                                            after
the name-taking and the name-giving
                                            with
tomorrow stretched out to swallow them
with questions
                    what could they keep

it is nowhere
recorded or remembered
who first spoke of home
(or what it could be now)
how the journey was begun
(or where it would end now)

what happened to the gifts

which story was agreed upon
(or how they knew it would be needed)
to tell the child when
                            (late some night
in a future that had been stolen from them
by stars that once briefly seemed to sing)

they would call him   and he turned
(as each child must)   to look at them
with unknown eyes

1.   (christopher :: william)
christopher is my sister's child. christopher william.
and william is his great-grandfather. william christopher.
i knew him. he was born on christmas day

2.   *(old)*
christopher is new. in our family the youngest
in years is always new. to be grown by everyone.
to be told and shown in stories years that everyone
old saw and remembers. christopher remembers me.
i remember william. and so we are known.

3.   *(but not for william)*
he sometimes runs to the door looking for me.
sometimes the door opens and i come through it.
sometimes he waits. waiting is new for christopher.
but not for william.

4.   *(then she is new and she remembers)*
high born. born high. carried high by everyone so that
he could be shown what is known. and what is new.
laura is known as the wife of william   is old until
she sees christopher. then she is new and she
remembers. he has his eyes.

5.   *(laura knows this)*
we are seldom known by what we see recognizing
is not knowing. laura knows this. she recognizes
death and christopher and she knows the difference.

6.   *(this is what she remembers)*
christmas is the difference between every christmas and
william to be told and shown to christopher. when
he tells us and shows us that he knows it will be
new. this is what she remembers. she waits to tell william.

7. *(and he was carried high on christmas through a door)*
when christopher tells us that he knows we will remember
that it was new when william told us. and he told us
all. he had laura for the telling and he was carried
high on christmas through a door   a world of doors
every door that stood the telling.

8. *(who was born on christmas)*
jesus comes into this now. now everyone remembers. who was
born on christmas. everyone who remembers was born on
christmas.

9. *(seldom known are the shadows until he can remember*
the smell and sound and the grip of hands around
his waist swinging him up with laughter)
of course the door we open for christopher is old.
seldom known are the shadows until he can remember
the smell and sound and the grip of hands around his
waist swinging him up with laughter.

10. *(did the hills laugh)*
did the hills laugh. laughter is as old as the hills.

11. *(presents always bring laughter and scrambled heaps of*
paper)
over this is the memory. and each wrapped present. christopher
brings william and laura a present. he has their eyes and
their laugh. presents always bring laughter and scrambled
heaps of paper.
                 he was always there.
                                    sometimes behind the door
sometimes opening it for us. if you cannot remember that what
is the use of knowing and telling it again and telling it
again will you know it and remember it it is remembering
christmas
remember that brought us to this door where christopher
stands waiting for me and william and a world that is as yet
for him as new as laughter and told again when she recognizes
his eyes and the surprise of a life before him.

12. *(that a child knows)*
and as he steps through the door she hands him
a life kept freshly wrapped in her mind seeing
in his young eyes the memory that a child knows.

13. *(william and christopher)*
a child (william) (christopher) knows that again
christopher is william and each of us tells him
that we remember now we remember and we knowing
know that
                the one who is to come is here.

14. *(with jesus. laughter)*
it has something to do with jesus it has some thing
to do with laughter.   some thing and everything to
do with jesus. any child can see. who knows. and so
it is known

SAUL'S DAUGHTER

"Michal the daughter of Saul...saw King David leaping and dancing before Yahweh and she despised him in her heart..."

(2 Sam. 6:16)

The scribbling dogs pretended a chronicle
of your deeds wherein I live a bitter woman
who laughed deriding your foolish ways

had I been given a spear   sweatsoaked naked
wonder
            it would have found what Saul my father
sought
            your heart

                        nor was he mad with prophecy
as they describe it   the howling came like acid
he drank each time you curved your spine
into the music
                        holding that ungainly harp like
the breath of God
                        but you were ever negligent
of the eyes which were your true anointing
the old fool Samuel pushed you into sunlight
when   seeing   the sweat and oil of sheep
he stumbled to touch you   mumbling   fate

every stone in your sling since then has killed
me

your curse came not because of my laughter
radiance of Israel   promise of the people
a sun unto yourself   leaping   thrusting
into the air of God   glistening with frenzy
you have found the safest lover of your life

what denial could not do I cannot care

Saul went mad when Jonathan became your harp
played and feathered by your breath
Saul went mad with hope
                              thinking I would be
the vessel of your pride
let Michal be one night of Jonathan and I am
satisfied
                  and I was
                              that one night of Saul's
pretending peace

again he hurled a spear   wanting yours
to cut him clean and aching

the women and the boys say you ravaged the sky
in weeping Jonathan's farewell
                                    no one spoke
of joy   locked inside the hungry daughter
of mad Saul the prophet   king   late of Israel

I had seen your cursing eyes enough by then
to know I lived secure
                              the princess   queen
of Israel will not weep because of dust
flung into her face
                        by your hot and stinking
dance
          Michal will be remembered
                                    it was I
who turned your song to the sword my hands
would pull

your God who needs the souvenirs of men
to feed his vengeance
                              has all of you now

stand there trembling   David of the harp
the music of your heart is his   your blood
his

the milk of your hot beauty
no one need
love you more

and the blood and flesh of Jonathan and Saul
are mine
beyond you by your truth
I despise
myself no more

AN AGONY : IN A GARDEN

I

For hours we sat there
                              desperate to catch his mind
knowing the meal would be bitter beyond forgetting

I did not
            know this
this man
                this beautiful hand and voice
and whispered words
                       that my glutton heart gorged on
this moving   laughing   shouting flame of love
this I knew   but did not
no, I lie
              I knew this   and all
                           we were betrayed
he was slandered
                He they called blasphemer
                              the shy son
who drank his mother's heart dry
                     the friend
who called his death closer with each undoing of hunger
twisted limbs soiled names
                    each gathering of the lost

II

I am lost
           more than when I pushed him into anger
more than when I doubted he would hold me fast through all
the storms that shattered my hope
                     But here we were
surrounded
           by a poison so foul and full   the air

could drown us
           all of us knew
                  they would use a daggered
lie to sever him from all he ever freely offered
                        would knot us into coldness
darkness   night folded into night

We knew it no longer counted
and we tumbled onto a stone where
Isaac the son was finally to be ripped apart

So I drew the foolish sword and claimed   justice

here is the reason to kill
            us all
we know   we redeem your lie by our gasping
need
       with this swift sundering
                now your guilt
is baptized by fury

We knew it was the end

          And then he turned
the wheel
       Put your sword back

I will not lose a single one

Ripped   dissolved   undone
             I will
stand here believing what I could never see
                He
saved us
      to see   he did not choose to be
the one who saves

III

I let the sword fall

                heavy as my shame

                                this

is what he saved me   to know   to

see

       to weep   to forever care

PETER : THE GALILEE ENCOUNTER

for the vows of Grant Garinger

When we first met his mother
                    she dismissed
his fear as nothing more than
                    crumbs upon
her gown

As we collected all that was left
to litter the hillside
                    we were blanketed
by the satisfied murmurings of
                    the greedy crowd
and turned to see
                    He had disappeared

When I awoke that blooded evening
                        foolish
guilty   and ashamed   I heard him

sighing
        "I would not drink"

                    "I cannot drink"

And my tears stirred the others

                    Now
on this day of sunlight surprises
and miraculously blue horizons
                    He
has looked at me
            for what I know
is a closing door

And said

You are the cup

        and they are thirsty

Now I know

        His yes

6 April 2008

THE SHORE : PETER REMEMBERS

I

The days choked me
no place we walked
no tree
      no well
no wall could keep
the wound from searing
bleeding
      so when brother
said
      let us take the boat
and seek fish

it was automatic

I can do that and not think
and I kept thinking
      we all did

nothing remained but
our amputated hearts

where
can we go
      sailing Tiberias
sea is
      nowhere far enough

II

The voice stopped us
confused the sense of time
dream-like we cast nets
as we were bid
      and when

the weight was inescapable
I knew
oh God, I knew   oh God
I knew that I had lied
all along
        I had not quit
the shores of hope
            I had not
sailed into despair

I knew

and found breath
to leap toward the voice

III

He handed me the food
and forced my eyes
into his
        what was left of
love

I shook

my body embarrassed me
with its
        stiff response

(not here   not now)

and I trembled

what
is left to love
        and I
wept for all the lies I had lived

what is left

IV

to love   to crawl out
of the cave of my own shame

to push myself onto
a scaffold of my own devising

to love   to feed   to
leap when I am called
into air   into nothingness

he handed me a meal
and told me to feed
them until
              there is nothing
left to love

it will
be

enough

IV

RESPONDING : A BLUES AESTHETIC

for Richard J. Powell and the Rev. Myron Taylor

Consider the varieties: there is a blues attitude, a blues feeling a blues
experience. A blues—if you think about it—aesthetic. What a mighty
hypothesis. Do the blues artists think about what they are doing?
                                                                    Even
before they begin the doing of it? If not, then we have to believe that
the first note out of Koko Taylor's throat hit the money with no devi-
ation from the intended arc. We would then have to believe that the music
just flows from B. B. King's fingers.
                        The autistic (formerly *idiot*) *savant*
always lurks in the high grass of anthropology.
                                        How do these unschooled
Beings manage to create such wonderful art!?!
                                    The answer: hard work
is often accomplished in learning environments not licensed by the State
Board of Education. After all, that organization is an economic arbiter,
Not a referee of the pedagogy of surviving in dis cold and friendless
world.
            How often does the amount of schooling have a direct correspondence
to the amount of money given or received for a piece of "wonderful" art?
No schooling: no money. An MFA? Top prices in the marketplace. It's
enough to make you want to sing (or paint or dance or write) the blues.

(Langston)
You 've taken my blues and
gone–
You sing 'em on Broadway
And you sing 'em in the   **(Jimmy Rushing, for one)**
Hollywood Bowl,   **Yeah. Well. . . I may be down,**
and you mixed 'em up with   **but I won't be down always.**
Symphonies   **I know the Sun's gonna shine**
And you fixed 'em   **in my backyard someday.**
So they don't sound like me.
Yep, you done taken my
blues and gone.

Emphasis added. Always added. That is one of the first requirements of the
blues. Add your emphasis to the sound of what everybody is feeling. The
Blues people are a dance people. Blues life is lived in the public square/circle.

Emphasis is rhythm. The raw material of drum music. Light soft heavy rapid
ponderous erratic: emphasis. All together now. Show me some attitude.

[**Response**]
        Aw, man, give me a challenge that's hard.

A challenge that is hard? How about . . . a situation where
somebody:

       (said Sterling Brown]
       dragged you from homeland chained you in coffles
       huddled you spoon-fashion in filthy hatches sold you to give a
       few gentlemen ease:

can you stand up to that with a stance that is attitude pure
and cold   stonecold simple and clean:

   you laugh   you sang   you shouted
you handed the memory on   in fact the term kinesthesis had
to be carved out of the aether just to squeeze all your
rhythms together   make it sound respectable-like
the goldchained necks are stiff   the sullen faces are masks of
the uncertain
                terror is also in the eye of the beholder

slunghipped and solid the young men spray words   become
the guerilla
              warriors of the blues future   being born in a public way gives
the body a certain obligation to add to the eyeballing

pose, hieroglyphic posse: then shift   a swing it and
dip   swing it and dip   bop till you drop spin and float and
swing and swing some more   you your daddy's child all the
way back to them times when nobody wanted your daddy to
know he had a child
              back to the real
Blues Time

you have to cut the air with a body blade my man
the funk of the summer and the collard greens
and the hot grease for the spicy chicken
and the tickling smell of cold beer breathed from windows
and porches and blue-black alleyways

the pain is there and memory chews on your eyelids and
lips the sound you remember coming to you as you were
muffled in your grandmama's lap at New Bethel Baptist
Church   and when you pushed up to breathe he was frozen there

Reverend Taylor pointing at the roof and holding the Bible
sweat running all over his suit shoulders and the choir wasn't
moving and grandmamma wasn't moving though her heart was
faster than before
                              there he was frozen   and looked like a statue
of an angel or a soldier and every body waited   seeing him
hanging in the middle of the air   you had to cry   seeing a
man hanging in the air   talking about pain and looking so
good while he did it

so many of our men have hung in the air
and it looked like the hell it was
in the real Blues time

we got to make it look good

I know my wings gonna fit me well
I tried them on at
the gates of Hell

and my robe   and my crown
but oh   especially
my wings

the blues hero never kills herself
the blues hero dies cause life squeezes him closed finally
but the blues hero cannot take his own life
squander it gamble it drink it smoke it shoot it spill it
away

yes

but inflict the killing blow
no

the point is to stand on the crossroads where the devil grins
with the face of God gleaming on his palm
the point is to stand cool at the gates of the nasty and the un-

acceptable

the point is to point to the truth
straight no chaser
the point is the point   yes
is the word
yes baby   yes daddy   yes mama   yes oh lordy yes
how can you teach somebody to die

when the blues is about grinding one more hour of life out of
the sweat and the singing and sweet taste of honey
split that rock
with a yes

attitude is all its spozed to be
passed on to me

passed on to you
on   the   point

AT THE BARBERSHOP I

(Shane)

Somebody open the door a minute

the boy smell like old bacon
                                    no
it's more like a bad toothache

I wanted to take him home and clean
him up
            then I thought about my car

and I just don't know

shove him into water and he just
might go back to his old ways
                                    and get
lost for too long

him and that dog (always some dog)
he says they are driving to Key West
to pick up a delivery
                        (by the time they
get to Georgia the dog gonna want to
take the bus the rest of the way)

you see him out there
                        pushing or pulling
his way into worlds that none of us
have ever heard of

We all our brothers' keepers
but I don't know

that smell

I just don't know

maybe next week

BARBERSHOP II

20 inside another 4 outside   late October heat wave
and a Friday morning
                          the clock wanders to the next
hour   and its tide pulls the sound from conversation
to oracle pounding football and baseball
                                              speculating
claiming and measuring size

the C. I. A. and the F. B. I. could fill their quota in this one
barbershop
                  it breaks your heart to see such razor wielding
under-used and sucked away by the dearly stressed
air-conditioner

                          no one has a thing to say about
the police busting open Daryl's skull last week
                                                          or
the girl who was found at the bottom of the hill
by her daddy
                  when the same damn police said
they never saw her body when they searched

the tide pulls back   10 minutes have disappeared
and the outcome of the playoffs has been

certified

              somebody ought to clean the rest-
room at least once a day
                              'cause the little boys
are learning to aim

BARBERSHOP III

The way he walked in   told us
he carried the smell of who
                              he used to be
        like a blanket protecting him
from the cold eyes and cutting
questions

                  He's been home
(that's the smell that invests
his smile: home)
                        about
two weeks

and is looking
for a game
                  his own eyes
quick like crickets in high
grass
          turn the barbershop
into the place where he made
himself
              the long-ago invincible wall

Youngblood   he says you done
got old and tired
                        what are you
about 25 or 26?
                    Yeah, you done
slowed down real bad
                            let's see
what you can do
                    tonight
                              I'll
give you a little juice

just be myself

                    go up like a 50
year old man
                and land
                            on my
feet

else I'll have to stay
                        here
and go to picking up

cans

BARBERSHOP : AUGUST MORNING

A good morning   early in the heat and rain
maybe six boys   and men   watching
women shoot for gold in a faraway
game
          a line here   a joke   and
some razor-quick stabs to the blues
of the day
                and the barber in the
baseball cap points his brush at me

already?

When it's your time
                    it's your time

young   young
so very young   man
                    say that and make
me go straight home and check my
policies

              how does it
                    feel (he said)
to get your beard trimmed
by the grim
              reaper

                    I feel
the day getting colder

even as

we laugh

CANE RIVER POEMS

for Wilfred Delphin

I. Catch A Fire–

Out there
in the backyard
              with air so
smelly it could make you drunk
(I know   Daddy give me a sip of his
drink lots of times. It's sweet
and snappish. "Like your Mama,"
he said. And laughed. Real nice.)

Big Mama and Uncle Junior and
me
       we were just sitting on the steps
and she said
                Sonny, catch a fire-
fly, son
          flicker ain't never as good
as flame

But get on out there and start
now
       and let them collect

Go on, he said
never wait

cause nothing else will

II. To Call You As Air

No one knew I left the room
the children were multiplying like
the amoeba they used to be
                              challenging
every chair   vase   instep   and eardrum
to survive their trajectories of excess

and all those intimately connected to each
other slipped into the satisfied coma we
always have for dessert when Christmas
finally wreaks its vindication at our Cane River
table
            I wanted to see what the silence looked like
in the dark
                  the half-lidded moon was isolated
in the blue black stillness

the bayou was quiet of all the hums   groans and
liquid murmurs of the season
                                          and a star slid toward
the earth just when I called you up
                                          as a cold airy touch
on my skin

oh Sweet Jesus in the morning
somebody said

                        and the star seared my heart

oh breath be full   oh ache be warm

may these children never know
how quick the darkness drinks

III. Listening For Dreams

He remembered his running to the grass
the summer he was nine

                      the long stretched-
out clouds   the dragonflies   frogs   and bees
hiding from the thunder and glass

                           which lined
the hallway his soul traveled in the houses
stores   schoolrooms   and the strange coldness
of the eyes that searched him raw and naked

the running was almost as good

                        as the hiding
in the grass

          almost as good as being
the only one   anywhere   he could see

so he could do the little boy acts   only now
remembered   never told   or claimed
where shame

             and fear   and foolish delight
being sweaty   and dusty   and full of secrets
were enough to fill a day

                Until now

I will know   he said   that this will stay

my feet

        my feet   are here   and here

I will draw my line   hide this plot   and
plan

     nothing

          no house   no road no
sign

       but deed my dreamgrass

              where some

other
listening boy   hiding in a man

can wrestle himself free

AND THE PETALS FALL

for our children everywhere

And when the rain warm dirt-filled
and heavy finally finishes its medication
of the day
                    a path is formed from
the petals of the crepe myrtle trees
banding us about as geographer's poles
not for shade but for certainty

we crush the bright pink flowerets
making an obscene stain

we come from the unsubsiding heat
we come from the traffic of pathless lives

drawn by the guidance of amber and green
dragonfly angels
                    we come laughing like drums
and with incense and fear

we sweep the streets with our eyes casting
about for the bits and pieces that could tell us
who has come before
                    and how they fared
and we leave scratched lines   marks   upon the soiled
concrete desperate that the late ones
                              the least ones
the lost ones will find the grains we have dropped
from hope

tear the garments you need not wear
go naked in the sweltering sun

                              rend the clothes
that soak up sweat and tears

our children are not living to survive
us
        and it was not rain

the crepe myrtle weeps before
and upon
us

IN YOUR GAZE I STAND

[In homage to "Miss Rosie," by Lucille Clifton]

when I can't look anywhere
else when the red light hangs on and on
when the Puerto Rican kids in the next lane
announce to the world that the beat will
take over the street
                              my eye falls on
you
           old lady with the twisted legs
and twisted fingers
                              trying to make it
across the street

across the street
across every street
old woman
                    I see you pushing all of us
who are ashamed now to move
                                        like music and
water

I look at you
and I will
tell you
when I can breathe again

that in your gaze
I stand up

A PRAYER FROM THE HEART

for Marcus Thomas: 2006

When a boy is born around
these parts
                seems like everybody
and her mama holds they breath

feeling the heart beating   the throat
closing shut
                the eyes straining not
to see the future

hoping against the storm
                        we smooth the skin
making our fingers learn a memory for when

we are going to wish for skin to love
for eyes to blow the grit from
                         for

shoulders to clutch and caress
for dreams to feed our prayers into

the boy was running from something
and running to somewhere
                     that is all
we have ever known

my fingers would have caught him
if I could

            now all we got is a story that
makes no sense
              and fingers that hurt to hold

just one more time

THE SUN WHISPERS, WAIT

for Rick Abert

I.

For three mornings the rain clicks
itself into my sleep
                          the ground has grown tired
and closed its pores   rejecting the assault

walk close to buildings   or not
                                        the rain does
not care

II.

Not a hand to touch
                        to point   to clarify
no lips to hush twisting   choking breath

fevers surge unabated
                          the fourth morning's rain
seeps inside me
                  the ache is now beyond bone

within my throat   behind my eyes
fist to heart
                  remembering
not a hand can stretch
so far
          as to reach heaven and hold the water back

III.

How does one notice someone leaving

when the skin remembers clearly
the soft hand banishing fear's cold delirium

the mouth still tastes candied
silences distracting the nightmare shocks

that waited our drifting minds
                              fingers
hold   forever
in the nerves with which the muscles
wrap and tie our first stumblings

I strain to feel some breeze
lifting the fog
the veil

and something whispers

wait

INTO A CLIMB

for Pete

when we arrived at the campsite
a deep whisper came into our voices
there at the west face of teewinot
where the gros ventre had hunted
eagles and starved themselves into
warriors   you guided me   at last
into your father's world
                          it was
as if the shock of hard rock
faces   and silences   and the final
ascent became your father   while
the mountains took his failings
into their slides and decaying
peaks
         into a climb you
started at the age of five   past
the treeline and glaciers   we look
where the high country is flat
yellow dust   where the country
who is my father sits untended
without words or whispers

SOME WINTER NIGHT

The traditional lore and craft tells
to prune the perennial bushes and trees
just before the bright hard spurts of spring growth spread wild

But I have waited   once again
until autumn's first cold round moon

the roots will be congested
the soil souring acid will salt the cauldron's lip
iron leeches dirt   squeezes the white tangled source

how does the earth evaporate
when water is withheld

how does the green continue its demand
for bark break and split
                              for leaf to breathe

I must cut away the brittle stalk and branch
where there is only knot   and the leaves
left yellow   dry   and jagged from
the mites and borer who must eat
the living to live

I may need the larger root
some winter night

THE SPACES LEFT ME

At night lately some small thing's hunger
roots and rips among the garbage
I have forgotten at my back door
I am not able just now to shore
up the property
                  maintain the standard
purity of my desires

the windows are left cracked
the door latch loose
old papers collapse in mounds

tomorrow I will buy a magic box
which will name and number all my
intrusions

and nothing   no trace no
scar   or scrap of you will be found

what displaced predator prowls
here   and how hungry will it become
before

I have cleaned all the spaces left me